HAL•LEONARD

UKULELE PLAY ALONG

Folk Pop Rock

CONTENTS

Ukulele by
Chris Kringel

ISBN 978-1-4584-2485-3

HAL•LEONARD®
CORPORATION
7777 W. BLUEMOUND RD. P.O. BOX 13819 MILWAUKEE, WI 53213

Visit Hal Leonard Online at
www.halleonard.com

UKULELE NOTATION LEGEND

THE MUSICAL STAFF shows pitches and rhythms and is divided by bar lines into measures. Pitches are named after the first seven letters of the alphabet.

TABLATURE graphically represents the ukulele fingerboard. Each horizontal line represents a a string, and each number represents a fret.

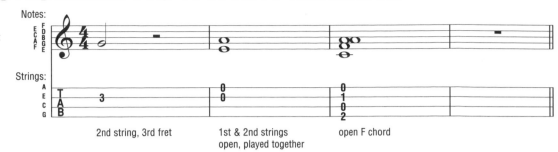

2nd string, 3rd fret   1st & 2nd strings open, played together   open F chord

HALF-STEP BEND: Strike the note and bend up 1/2 step.

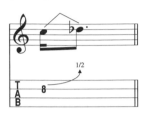

WHOLE-STEP BEND: Strike the note and bend up one step.

GRACE NOTE BEND: Strike the note and immediately bend up as indicated.

SLIGHT (MICROTONE) BEND: Strike the note and bend up 1/4 step.

BEND AND RELEASE: Strike the note and bend up as indicated, then release back to the original note. Only the first note is struck.

PRE-BEND: Bend the note as indicated, then strike it.

VIBRATO: The string is vibrated by rapidly bending and releasing the note with the fretting hand.

HAMMER-ON: Strike the first (lower) note with one finger, then sound the higher note (on the same string) with another finger by fretting it without picking.

PULL-OFF: Place both fingers on the notes to be sounded. Strike the first note and without picking, pull the finger off to sound the second (lower) note.

LEGATO SLIDE: Strike the first note and then slide the same fret-hand finger up or down to the second note. The second note is not struck.

SHIFT SLIDE: Same as legato slide, except the second note is struck.

TRILL: Very rapidly alternate between the notes indicated by continuously hammering on and pulling off.

TREMOLO PICKING: The note is picked as rapidly and continuously as possible.

NOTE: Tablature numbers in parentheses mean:

1. The note is being sustained over a system (note in standard notation is tied), or

2. The note is sustained, but a new articulation (such as a hammer-on, pull-off, slide or vibrato) begins, or

3. The note is a barely audible "ghost" note (note in standard notation is also in parentheses).

Additional Musical Definitions

 (accent) • Accentuate note (play it louder)

 (staccato) • Play the note short

D.S. al Coda • Go back to the sign (𝄋), then play until the measure marked "***To Coda***," then skip to the section labelled "**Coda**."

D.C. al Fine • Go back to the beginning of the song and play until the measure marked "***Fine***" (end).

N.C. • No chord.

 • Repeat measures between signs.

 • When a repeated section has different endings, play the first ending only the first time and the second ending only the second time.

TRACK 1

Annie's Song

Words and Music by John Denver

* Voc. hum 3rd time, next 18 meas.

To Coda

laugh - ter, _____ let me die in your
time, _____ like a walk in the rain, _

arms. _____
like a storm in ___ the
Let me lay down be - side _

des - ert, _____
like a sleep - y blue _
you, _____
let me al - ways ___ be
3. Let me give my life

o - cean. _____
with you. _____ }
You fill up my
to you. _____
2., 3. Come let me love _

sens - es, _____
come fill me ___ a -
you, _____
come love me ___ a -

gain. _____
gain. _____
2. Come let me

At Seventeen

Words and Music by Janis Ian

6. *See additional lyrics*

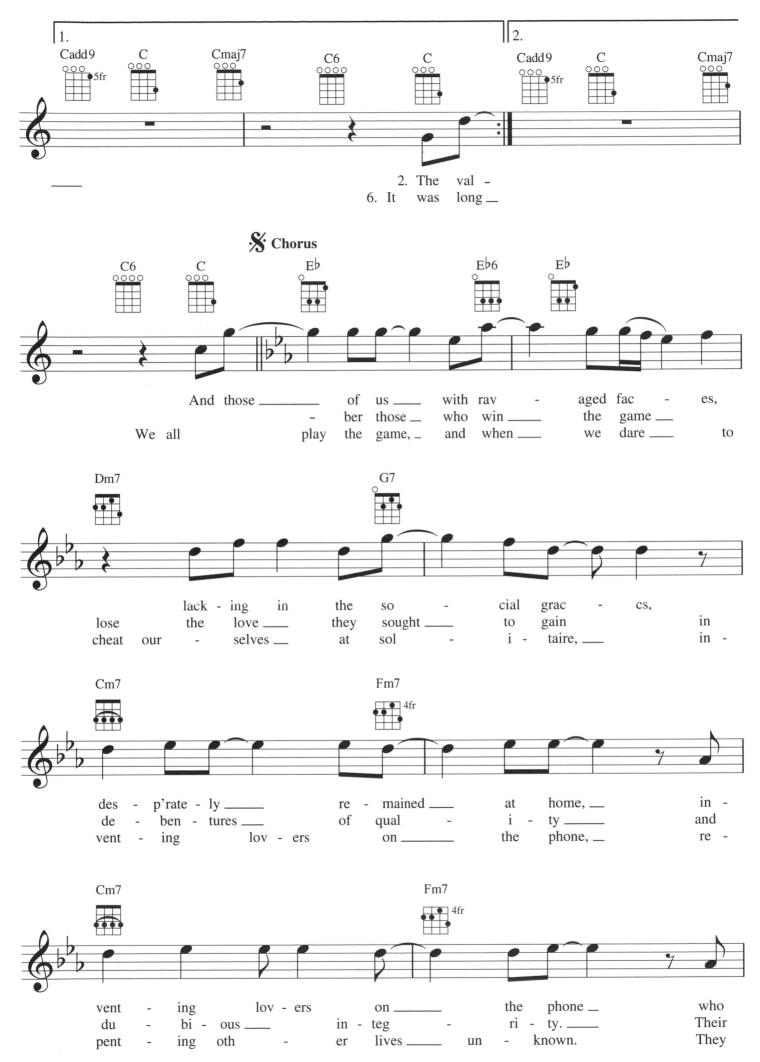

7

A♭

called to say, "Come dance ____ with me," ____
small town ____ eyes will gape at you ____ and dull ____
call and say, "Come dance ____ with me," ____

G7

Cm7

and mur - mured vague ____ ob - scen - i - ties.
____ sur - prise ____ when pay - ment due
and mur - mur vague _____ ob - scen - i - ties

Fm7

To Coda 1 ⊕

To Coda 2 ⊕ **G7**

Dm7

It is - n't all it seems ____ at sev - en - teen.
ex - ceeds ac - counts re - ceived at
at ug - ly girls like me ____ at

Verse

Cadd9 **C** **Cmaj7** **C6** **C**

3. A brown - eyed ____ girl in hand ____ me downs, ____
____ re - la - tioned home - town queen

Dm7sus4 **Dm7** **Dsus2** **Dm7**

whose name ____ I nev - er could ____ pro - nounce, ____
mar - ries in - to what ____ she needs, with a guar -

A Horse with No Name

Words and Music by Dewey Bunnell

TRACK 5

The heat was hot __ and the ground was dry, __ but the
Un - der the cit - ies _____ lies a heart made of ground _ but the

Chorus

air was full __ of __ sound. __ I've been through the des - ert on a
hu - mans will give __ no __ love. __ You see I've

horse with no name. _ It felt good to be out __ of the rain. __ In the

To Coda ⊕

des - ert, you can re - mem - ber your name _ 'cause there ain't no one for to

Interlude

give you no pain. _ La, la, la, ____ la, la, la, la, la,

1.   2.

la, la, la. _____ ____ 2. Af - ter

Verse

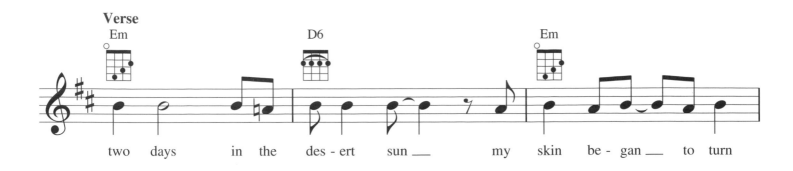

two days in the des - ert sun ___ my skin be - gan ___ to turn

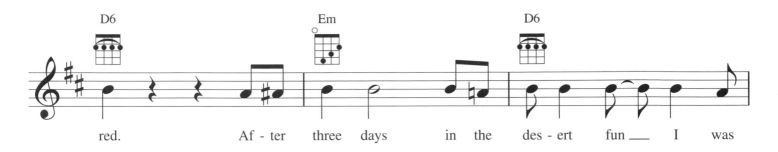

red. Af - ter three days in the des - ert fun ___ I was

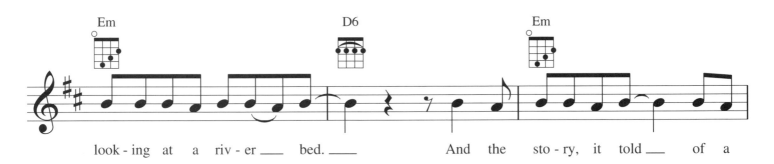

look - ing at a riv - er ___ bed. ___ And the sto - ry, it told ___ of a

riv - er that flowed _ made me sad to think _ it was dead. You see I've

Chorus

been through the des - ert on a horse with no name. ___ It felt

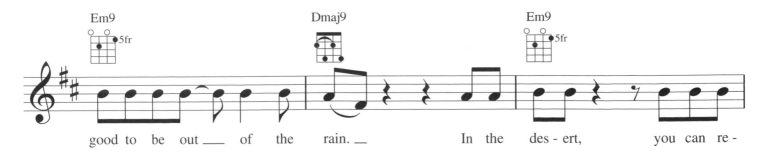

good to be out ___ of the rain. ___ In the des - ert, you can re -

I'll Have to Say I Love You in a Song

Words and Music by Jim Croce

TRACK 7

words just came out wrong. ___ So I'll have to say ___ I love ___

D.S. al Coda

___ ya in a song. ___ 3. Yeah, I

Coda

Outro

26 Miles
(Santa Catalina)

Words and Music by Glen Larson and Bruce Belland

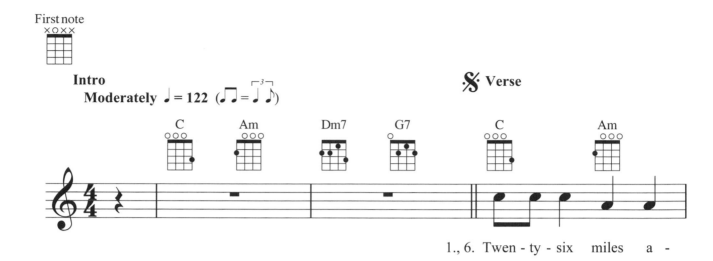

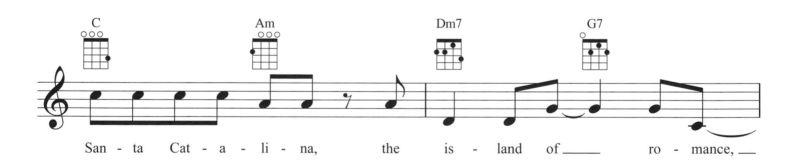

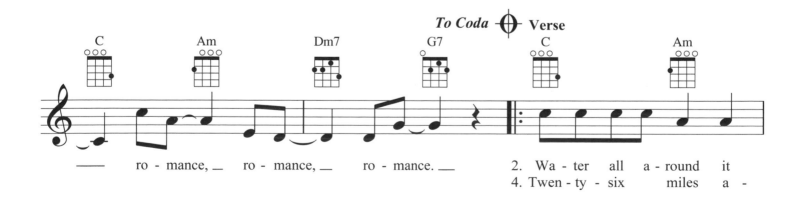

ev - 'ry - where, __ trop - i - cal trees and the salt - y air, __ but for
cross the sea __ San - ta Cat - a - li - na is a wait - in' for me, __

me the thing that's a wait - in' there's __ ro - mance. __
San - ta Cat - a - li - na, the is - land of _____ ro - mance. __

Bridge

It seems so dis - tant, twen - ty - six miles __ a - way,
A trop - i - cal heav - en out in the o - cean,

rest - in' in the wa - ter se - rene. _____ I'd work for an - y - one,
cov - ered with trees __ and girls. ___ If I have to swim, _____ I'll

e - ven the Na - vy, who would float me to my is - land dream.
do it for - ev - er till I'm gaz - in' on those is - land pearls.

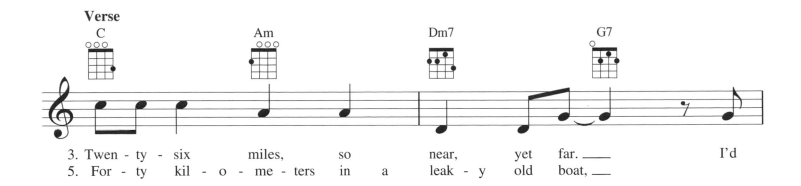

Verse

3. Twen - ty - six miles, so near, yet far. ____ I'd
5. For - ty kil - o - me - ters in a leak - y old boat, ____

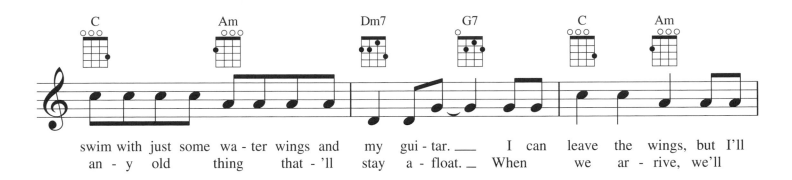

swim with just some wa - ter wings and my gui - tar. ____ I can leave the wings, but I'll
an - y old thing that - 'll stay a - float. _ When we ar - rive, we'll

2nd time, D.S. al Coda

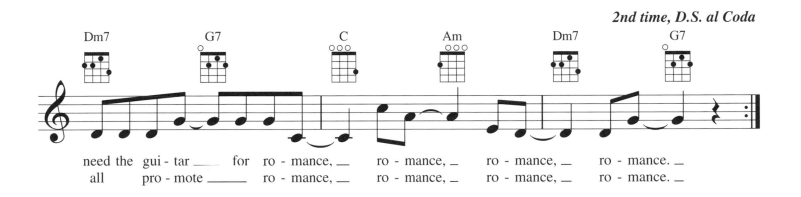

need the gui - tar ____ for ro - mance, _ ro - mance, _ ro - mance, _ ro - mance. _
all pro - mote ____ ro - mance, _ ro - mance, _ ro - mance, _ ro - mance. _

⊕ Coda
Outro-Verse

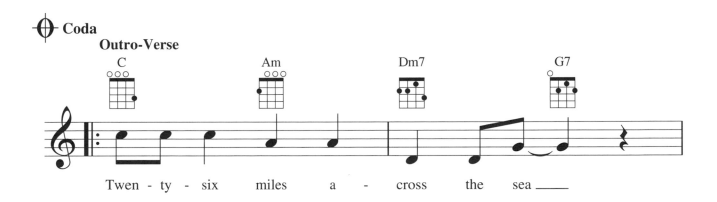

Twen - ty - six miles a - cross the sea ____

Repeat and fade

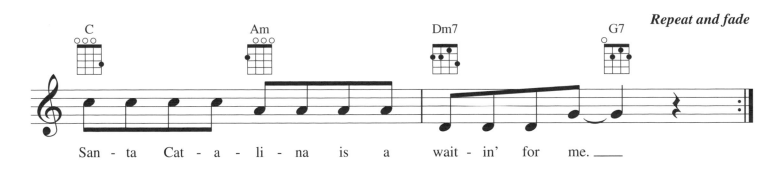

San - ta Cat - a - li - na is a - wait - in' for me. ____

Longer

Words and Music by Dan Fogelberg

I've been in love ___ with you. _____

I am in love ___ with you. _

Bridge

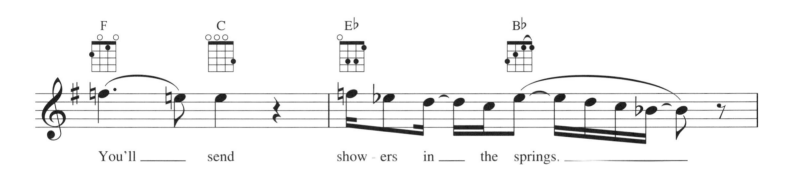

I'll _____ bring   fi - re in ___ the win - ters.

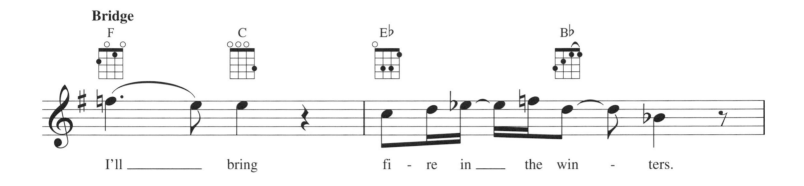

You'll _____ send   show - ers in ___ the springs. _____

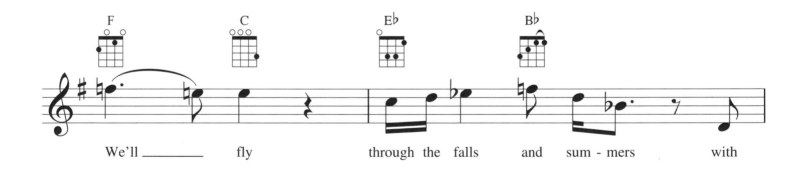

We'll _____ fly   through the falls   and   sum - mers   with

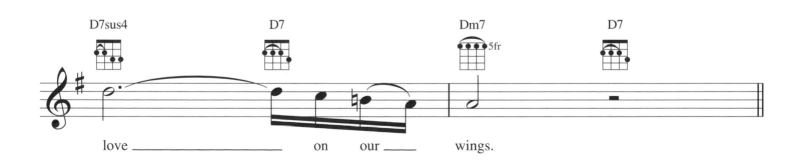

love _____   on our ___ wings.

Verse

3. Through the years, ___ as the fi - re ___ starts to mel - low, ___

burn - ing ___ lines in the book ___ of our ___ lives. ___ Though the

bind - ing cracks, ___ and the pag - es ___ start to yel - low, ___

I'll be in love ___ with you. ___

Interlude

I'll be in love ___ with you. ___

Play 3 times

TRACK 11

Nights in White Satin

Words and Music by Justin Hayward

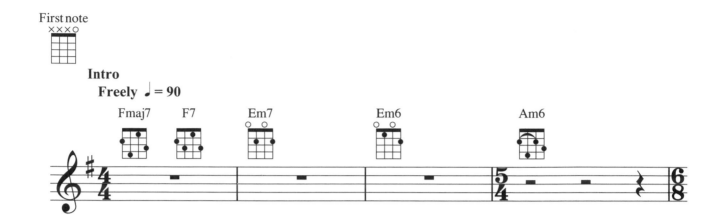

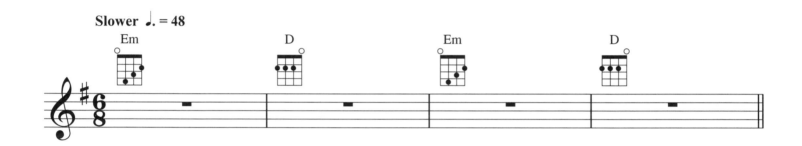

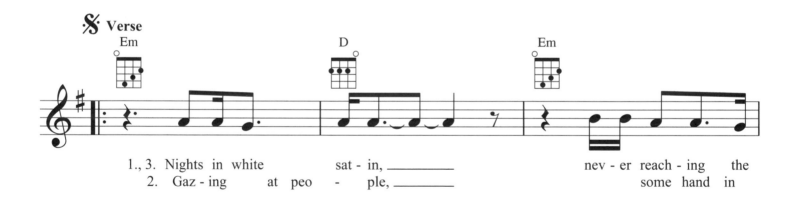

1., 3. Nights in white sat - in, _____ nev - er reach - ing the
2. Gaz - ing at peo - ple, _____ some hand in

end. _____ Let - ters I've _ writ - ten _____
hand. _____ Just what I'm go - ing _____ through

never meaning to send. _____
they can't under - stand. _____

Beau - ty I'd al -
Some try to tell _

- ways ___ missed
___ me _____

with these eyes ___ be - fore. _____
thoughts they can - not de - fend. _____

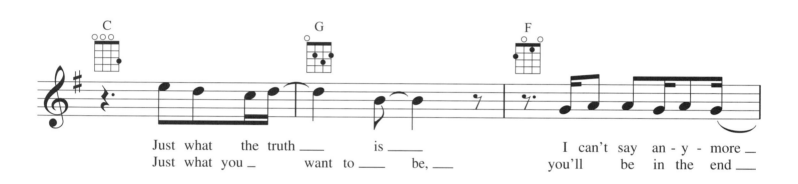

Just what the truth ___ is ___
Just what you _ want to ___ be, ___

I can't say an - y - more _
you'll be in the end _

Chorus

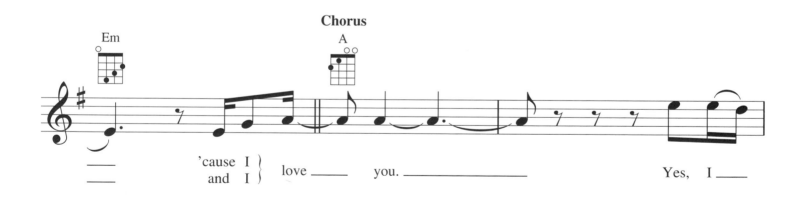

___ 'cause I
___ and I } love ___ you. _____

Yes, I ___

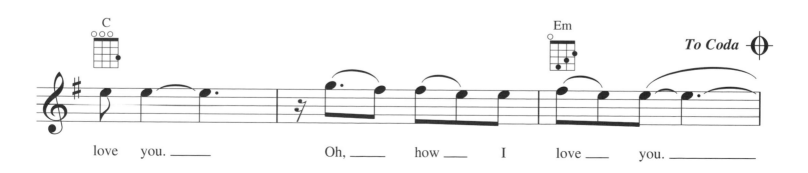

To Coda ⊕

love you. _____ Oh, ___ how ___ I love ___ you. _____

Oh, _____ how I love _____ you. _____

Flute Solo

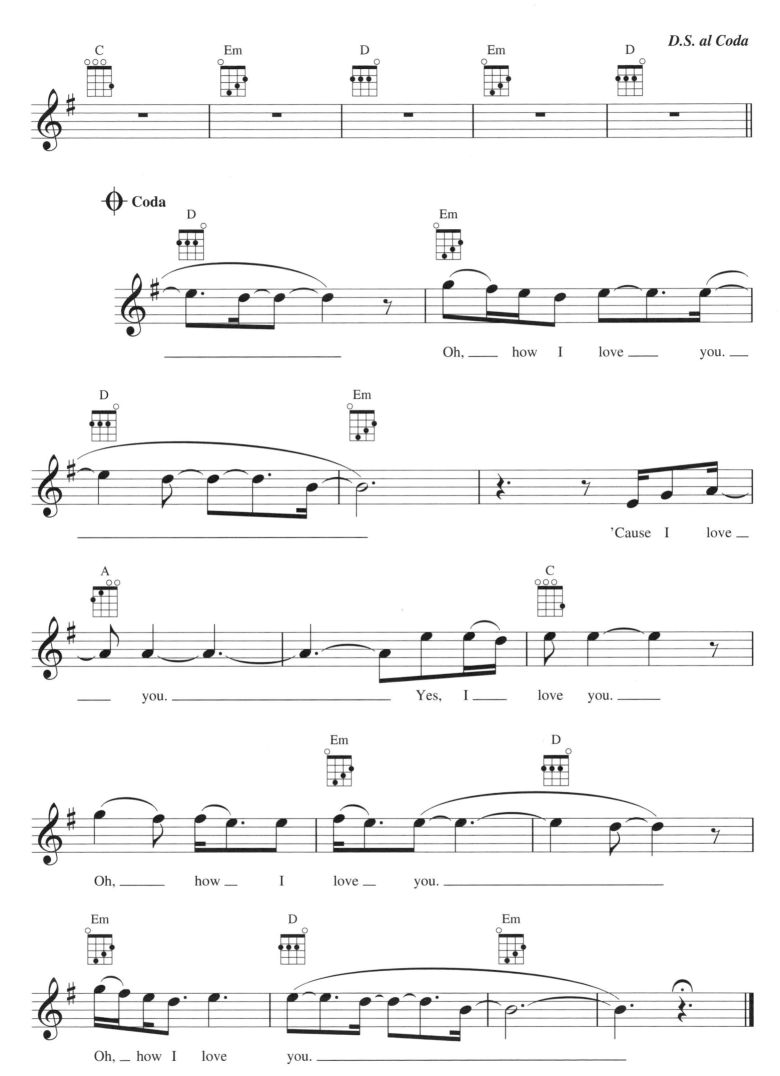

Oh, _____ how I love _____ you. _____

'Cause I love _____

_____ you. _____ Yes, I _____ love you. _____

Oh, _____ how _ I love _ you. _____

Oh, _ how I love you. _____

Suzanne

Words and Music by Leonard Cohen

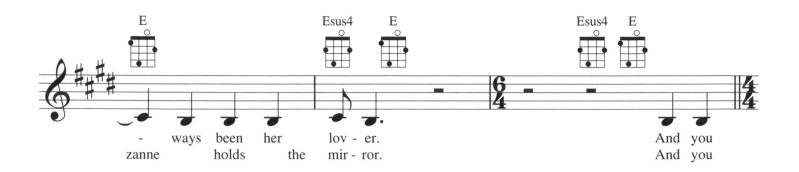

-ways been her lov-er.
zanne holds the mir-ror.
And you
And you

Chorus

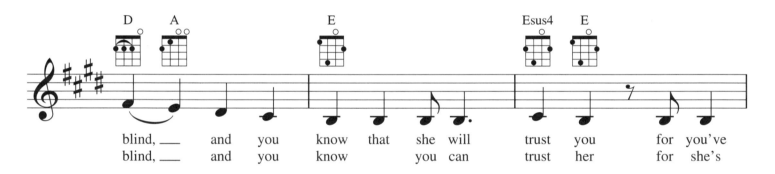

want to trav-el with her, and you want to trav-el
want to trav-el with her, and you want to trav-el

blind, ___ and you know that she will trust you for you've
blind, ___ and you know you can trust her for she's

To Coda 2 ⊕

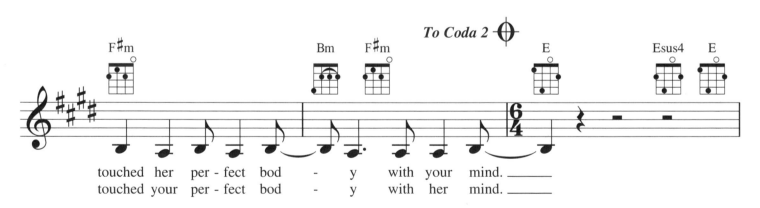

touched her per-fect bod — y with your mind. _____
touched your per-fect bod — y with her mind. _____

D.S. al Coda 1   ⊕ **Coda 1**

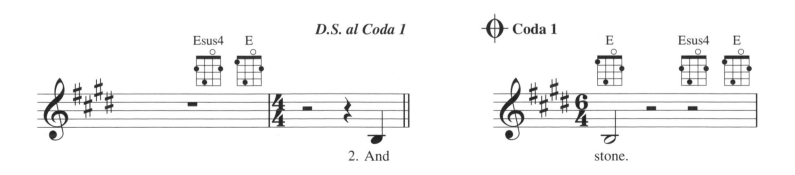

2. And
stone.

   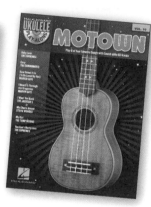